LONELY LONELY LONELY LONELY LONELY LONELY LONELY LONELY LONELY LONELY LONELY LONELY LONELY LONELY

Incredibly Lonely, That's Me

Written by Ben Keckler

Illustrated by Dick Davis

Creative Development by Diana Barnard

Eagle Creek Publications, LLC
PO Box 781166
Indianapolis, Indiana 46278

For all the wonderful people who appear to be content with life but feel the heartsong of loneliness.

Special thanks to the Bereavement Support Groups at Hendricks Regional Health and Kurt Wubbena.

--B.K.

Incredibly Lonely, That's Me
Text copyright © 2007 by Benjamin F. Keckler, III
Illustrations copyright © 2007 by Benjamin F. Keckler, III
Printed in the USA
All rights reserved
No part of this book may be used or reproduced in any manner whatsoever without written permission
except in the case of brief quotations embodied in critical articles and reviews. For information address,
Eagle Creek Publications, LLC, PO Box 781166, Indianapolis, Indiana 46278
www.eaglecreekpubs.com

Library of Congress Cataloguing-In-Publication Data
Keckler III, Benjamin F.
  Incredibly Lonely, That's Me/by Ben Keckler; illustrated by Dick Davis; artistic consultant Diana Barnard; 1st ed.
  p.   cm.
  Summary: A grieving child struggles to understand and accept the feeling of loneliness.
  ISBN 10: 0-9769093-2-4
  ISBN 13: 978-0-9769093-2-3
  [1. Stories in rhyme 2. Bibliotherapy 3. Self-help: Transition, Grief]

With thanksgiving for the life of Laura

Honoring the grief work of Melissa

This book is created especially
for you by a whole team of
people who want you to be
the best you can be.
Ben, Cheryl, Diana, Dick,
Mike, Kurt, Jan, Nevin and, of course,
Melissa have come together to bring you this
special story to help you when you feel
Incredibly Lonely.

We're thinking of you!

Come with me to my world,

The world where I survive.

Come with me to my world,

It lasts much longer than 9 to 5.

Come with me to my world, it's where I live all day.

Come with me to my world,
In my heart at work and play.

Come with me to my world,

A place I didn't think I'd ever know.

Come with me to my world,

And let all your feelings grow.

Come with me to my world,

A safe place where your insides are explored.

Come with me to my world,

A place where every heartbeat is lovingly adored.

Come with me to my world,
It may be your world, too.

Come with me to my world,

Where folks say, "You're just feeling blue."

Here in my world I deal with lonely all the time.

You see I lost my big sister when I was only nine.

She was a great security, in her I would confide.

I'll never know the "whys" of the day that Laura died.

She shared with me special secrets,

Which always made me glad.

If you get to know my folks,

PLEASE don't tell mom or dad!

SHHHHH

She had good values in her heart
And she was really brave.

Why did she climb and fall?
It certainly wasn't to misbehave!

I think she kept on reaching
For a challenge that was new.

Never did she stop and think of risk,
That isn't what teenagers do.

Now if you will come with me to my world,

I've got a lesson I want to tell.

It's something I might not have learned so quickly
If Laura hadn't fell.

If I can do this,
you can too!

Incredibly Lonely is my world each and every day.

I let the feeling come and go, I welcome it and let it stay.

Each time I listen closely, even lonely can give me hope,
To help me through those tough times when I can hardly cope.

Lonely visits anytime, even when surrounded

I can feel alone!

And surprise –

it can even come when I'm on the telephone!

When it comes and stays a bit, it's a feeling I now trust

Even if it makes me cry so many tears that I make iron rust!

As I listen to the lonely that is right here in my soul,

I feel a presence protect me when I'm going out of control.

When Incredibly Lonely comes your way

And curls you up into a ball,

Or takes you to some distant place,

Maybe even nails you to a wall,

Do not run away from it, please trust that it can be

A chance to unite you with the one
Who still lives eternally!

Yes, I miss my sister and I believe I always will

But even in my loneliness, she surrounds me still!

Life now is all about trusting in the hope that I will be

Peaceful and comforted – cause

Incredibly Lonely, That's Me

It's OK to feel lonely.

There is so much hope!

Yes, you can be happy!

Explore new feelings!

Love is always with you.

It's Your turn to Express Yourself

Loneliness is a feeling that lets us know we long for the company of others.

We want companionship to help ease our broken feelings. Our hearts seem to say, "Please listen to me as I share my story."

I think I will do something incredible today!

Lonely
Everyone feels Lonely for
me I feel Lonely at night
I'll toss and turn and begin to
cry. I feel Lonely at night
then I'll think My sister
use to be here to take
away the fear then I cry
more because she is here no more
but wait she is here in heart
all of my relatives have part to
heven they will stay there and
I will stay here but again
there've with me and my tears
at night are gone and it is
bright

by Melissa

One good way to express yourself is writing or journaling. One day Melissa wrote her feelings about her lonely times. Later she shared them with a listening friend and now she shares her feelings with you.

Take some time to **express yourself** and your feelings. You don't have to write about loneliness, maybe you'd like to express another difficult feeling you are experiencing.

Here is another opportunity to **express yourself**. The feeling of loneliness generally comes to us when we are feeling brokenhearted. Traveling in the world of loneliness begins to feel a bit better when we take time to claim values that are important to us.

Instructions:

1. Trace the heart onto a sheet of paper.
2. Cut the heart into 6 or 7 pieces.
3. Write an important value on each piece of the heart.
4. Share them with a listening and affirming friend.
5. Daily spend time developing (re-developing) each value.

Here are three ideas
(we don't want to give you too many -- we want you to write and name YOUR values):

1. I value the members of my family.
2. I value quiet time thinking about my loved one.
3. I value my pet.